Abominations of The Wilting Rose

Stephanie Rose Hold

BookLeaf Publishing

India | USA | UK

Abominations of The Wilting Rose © 2024
Stephanie Rose Hold

Presentation by *BookLeaf Publishing*

Web: www.bookleafpub.com

E-mail: info@bookleafpub.com

ISBN: 9789360947262

First edition 2024

ACKNOWLEDGEMENT

To my mother, thank you for being the first poet whose voice inspired mine. I have always marveled at the way you write and use your own voice. I have always appreciated the way your mind works, though I may be biased because it's quite similar to my own. Thank you for raising me in a way that allowed me to thrive as a writer, and for always caring and encouraging me forward. You made me the writer I am today, and the woman I am today. Without you walking all these same roads I would never have found my way.

To my sister, thank you for listening to me ramble about this endlessly. Thank you for being the first person to hear about every ridiculous idea I have and every roadblock that comes up along the way. Thank you for being someone I can always talk to and discuss my ideas, my hopes, and my fears with. I am glad that we are close enough both literally in space and emotionally to be able to talk every day and to always enjoy the company of. Without our days watching shows and discussing books I don't think I'd ever have found the inspiration I needed to write something like this.

To Professor Cosand, thank you for pushing me to write poetry. Thank you for putting me in a scenario where I could fall in love with this artform, and for being there when I first wrote a poem about monsters. I hope that you enjoy the pieces of my work from your class that stayed in my heart, and burrowed their way into this collection. I hope you can see your instructions in each poem, and that you're happy with the evolution that I've gone under. I am grateful every day that I was in your classes.

To Nikki, I owe you a lifetime of thanks. If my thanks were printed into a million copies of this page it wouldn't be enough. I would not have been able to do this without your support, your notes, and days of your time keeping me on the path to completing this project. I adore being in the trenches of frantic writing with you, and I will be grateful for this time for as long as I may live. Please never forget that without you, these pieces would never have taken this shape.

To Sophie, my love, thank you for being here while I wrote these pieces. Thank you for showing me sides of them that I'd have never seen, and enthusiasm that pushed me through my most exhausting days. Thank you for loving me as I deflated into nothing, and for inspiring me to be the best poet I can be every waking moment of my life. I hope that you're proud, and that you enjoy this collection. My work is for your eyes, and your heart.

Bloom

A rose was plucked from the gardens of the palace of The High Heavens. It was clutched in a desperate hand and filled with intention. The intention of one wracked with grief, of one on the verge of madness, of one who could see… and make others see. The rose's thorns were soaked in blood. The rose was made to drink of the divine. Overcome by Her essence, it twitched to life. It writhed with every one of its newfound limbs—spindly like a spider's, with thorns in place of hair. It strained with the eyes that emerged in the fold of each of its petals. It flexed its stinger, dripping with divinity—with the blood of its maker. The rose was alive, the rose was aware, and the rose was soaking up the desolate whispers of a Goddess.

The rose slid free from its maker's hand. It skittered down the garden path: past the palace, past every gate of The High Heavens, into The Realm of Mortals. It nestled itself in the soil of temples. It hid amongst roses planted in Her honor. The rose waited patiently for a head to present itself. It sat idly until knees touched its soil, until someone devoted closed their eyes and offered their neck in submission. Finally, the rose leapt with ferocity—with intention. The intention of one who could see… and make others see. It tread a bloody path across the shoulder of the devoted. It sprung past the hand that swept up in self defense. Its thorny legs curled comfortably into pierced cartilage as it latched onto its prey. Its stem weaved delicately through ear canals—it grew until its stinger found purchase in the worshiper's mind. At once they could see. They could see the ghosts of those struck down in the holy wars and the lingering spirits of gods. They could see the monsters born of the essence of divinity—born of The Goddess who had cursed them with understanding.

The devoted wandered, for a time. They screamed to anyone who would listen of demons and corrupting bile from The High Heavens. They ran from every town not already plagued by madness as their neighbors turned hostile. They ran out of warm places to sleep nearly as quickly as they lost their will to fight. The sight can only be given for so long. For all the gifts it forces upon its host, the blood of the divine is poison, and the devoted was doomed to die. The rose clung onto the body for as long as it was useful. Once the devoted had fallen, it searched for a new human to infect. It leapt between scholars and soldiers. It rode merchants into crowded markets. Eventually, the parasite found its way to me.

I had no idea the path I'd chosen when I knelt before a trampled flower. I had no idea what was happening as its thorns tore through me. Before I understood anything, I was forced to understand everything. I understood Her misery, Her isolation. I understood why The Goddess of Roses had birthed such a monster. I was overwhelmed by Her grief as I was the visions of beasts around every corner. It didn't take long to realize that no one would believe me, that frothing at the mouth about monsters and the rose curled around my ear would only end one way. And so I decided that I wouldn't say a word—that instead, I would take up the pen.

It is here that I will record the madness that ravages me.
It is here that I will share the details of the abhorrent things that waltz through our reality.
It is here that I will build a monument to The Wilting Rose—to The Goddess who will reside over this decaying world.

Muse

The Wilting Rose grew tired of isolation—of hearing Her own morbid thoughts echo across the palace of The High Heavens. Unheard, unanswered, unloved. Escaping its walls offered no remedy. All She saw as She strolled through Her emptied kingdom among the stars was charred and crumbling temples. She met no one but the buried gods who She loathed even above the thought of going mad. And so She thought to summon the Inspirations; the spirits of art, of expression, and the heart of creation. The only gods She'd found mercy for when Her wrath had met divinity's gates. She hosted them at Her court in The High Heavens, She drew them into the lowest chambers of Her home, and She butchered every one. She spared their lives—She desired every one of their souls—but of their bodies, She needed only one. One perfect Inspiration to remind Her of who She was before this place was empty. Of what She loved before the silence came.

She took one eye from the painter, and one from the sculptor. From the architect she pilfered an eye and an arm, both of which found themselves

stitched together in their new body's right
stump. From the singers, She took four mouths
for four descending tones. She placed them from
highest to lowest. The highest on its jaw, the
next on its breast, one at its abdomen's center,
and the lowest on its thigh. Legs of the dancer,
hand of the poet, hair from Heaven's beautician.
She gathered the most revered feature of every
Inspiration. She brought them together into one
flawless being, and into it she wept. She wept
memories of the flowers of her garden, of the
songs of rebellion, of everything She'd dreamed
of when She brought The High Heavens low.

And so Her perfect Muse stood before Her.
Three mismatched, glossy eyes stared vacantly
ahead: two in her head and one in her palm.
Three mouths chewed their way free of the tulle
of her gown to join the highest in anguished
wails. With legs that bled as they wobbled to the
rhythm that constantly played in her mind. With
tools held clumsily between each stitched up
finger on her arms of vastly different sizes. Her
bodice was soaked with the bloody tears of her
creator. Her skirt, ripped open by singer's teeth,
spun aimlessly after her wandering feet. Her
sleeves grew filthy from ink, and paint, and clay,
and anything else her Mistress had placed in her
hands. The Muse was set loose to make Heaven

beautiful. The Goddess of Roses, for a moment
rejuvenated, watched Her creation stumble off
rhythm into the streets. The Goddess was
pleased for only a day as she made a list of
requests. She was pleased for only a day as she
dreamed of refurbished towers and statues in the
image of those who'd died deserving one. She
believed for one blissful day that her joy would
be recaptured, and singing would once again
race through her ears.

The Goddess was returned to reality by the
sounds of four separate odes screamed in four
separate keys. She rushed to Her Muse to aid
Her, and to inspect the work of the previous day.
Statues had gibberish carved along their backs.
Temples were defaced by clumsy lines painted
in the blood of fallen gods. The Muse danced in
the wreckage it created. It danced without pause
even as shards of marble dug into its feet—even
as it grew filthy in the mess of art it no longer
knew how to make. The Goddess of Roses
began to wilt again. Her heart sank and Her tears
seared the ground. She could fix it, if only She
could get her to hold still, if only she would stop
screaming. But She could not quiet Her creation.
She could not tame her or give her purpose. She
could not do anything but make it suffer.
Perhaps it was panic that led Her to cast Her

Muse from Heaven—or perhaps it was rage. Whatever the reason, She flung the thing away. She sent it to anywhere that wasn't home, anywhere where she needn't be reminded of her kingdom's decay.

The creature found herself in our world, in the realm of mortal artists. She was cursed to wander aimlessly—to dance along unlit roads until the tones of music well performed caught her ear and drew her to a tavern. Until a minstrel's performance compelled her to follow the artist home and pry off their ears. She lurks wherever she feels the vibrations of song, wherever she smells paint, wherever she hears the dreams of the artists she longs so desperately to be. She appears to them in private moments. She sings to them in maddening tones, she carves poems into their flesh. Anyone who catches her attention—who proves worthy of her Mistress of Roses, she takes apart to one day bring home.

Amalgamation

The Goddess was plagued by abominable
thoughts. It was the sensation of molasses
spilling and coating one's brain. Her mind was
clouded with doubt, unrest, and terror as these
thoughts began to fill Her head and press against
Her skull. Too tight. Too heavy. Too much. She
employed ancient tonics from the shelves of
heavenly alchemists but found no relief in them.
She used Her own divine powers to attempt to
sate the worries, or to boil them away, but even
with all Her might She could only make them
thrash within Her. All She could feel day and
night was the weight of these intruders—the
pain of their constant writhing in Her skull. She
could think of nothing else. Every waking
moment was dedicated to destroying them
before they could destroy Her. In a final moment
of desperation, The Wilting Rose opened Her
skull, and allowed these abominable thoughts to
slip away. Ichor, thick and dark, slipped from
Her mind—enough to fill a pond. The Wilting
Rose paid no mind to the wretched thing that
formed in this pool of worries. She gave it no
further attention as it gathered into an ooze and

slipped away from the palace of high heaven. It was finally over, She had finally freed Herself.

None can say what happened to the congealed thoughts of The Goddess, but there is a legend. A legend of a dark star crashing down from the Heavens some years ago. A legend of a massive, oozing thing limping away from the crater. A legend that the Earth in its path rotted away and the forest screamed for mercy with its approach. Whether the ooze found a corpse to suit its size, or it changed the fauna to suit its needs, no one could ever know. All that is known is that the ooze went in, and not long after, a new terror revealed itself to the villages surrounding the forest.

An amalgamate beast with the ever-gyrating body of a jungle fowl—if a jungle fowl could rival taverns in size. Its body is covered in feathers caught mid molt; they carry the blue-gray color of a freshly rotting corpse, with taloned feet that stamp against the ground ceaselessly. Its wings flutter and flap with the force of stormy winds and blow its feathers in every direction. Its face is that of a mosquito—as if an insect hatched from the neck of a chicken to overtake its face. Its proboscis—dripping with a thick, dark ichor—practically drags across the ground the way it angles down to poke at anything that may draw blood. It has the eyes of a spider, ever blinking, watching every angle. Insectoid legs sprout along the featherless spine that leads down to its tail. The telltale sign of its approach is the chittering of a dozen insects the size of one's arms ringing from the forest. Its tail is long and barbed—like the stinging creatures that glide along the forest river's bottom. As its body rushes frantically across the countryside, the barbs of its tail dig into the ground. They hook into roots and soil, infecting everything in its path with the same rotten bile that drips from its face. The same rotten bile that flows through its veins.

Assault from the Amalgamation is swift. It stomps through the villages around its forest for only a day or two. Its talons crush through farmhouses and flatten would-be warriors hoping to circumvent its attack. Its proboscis sinks into livestock, bags of feed, anything that catches its eyes as it stumbles down the road. It pierces through village guards to inspect the barns that lie behind them. But the initial rampage is brief; the real trouble is what appears in its trail. Anything the beast touches during its visit changes. Its tail spreads the holy word of decay; anything that grows in the trenches it makes in the soil warps. Produce grows bloated and quivering. It becomes a conduit of accursed bile, and anyone or anything whose teeth sink into it is damned. Animals become venomous killers: their horns and claws grow until they curl, their mouths leak with the same ooze as the one who remade them. Humans who consume it become mounds of boils and insects. They wander in agony until they burst, spreading the infection to their neighbors. Even once the creature leaves, these villages are unable to breathe. Even once the Amalgamation has forgotten them, they must live in its aftermath forever.

Growth has all but ceased in the villages along the forest's edge. Their foe has no pattern, and it moves with no intelligence. It simply rushes at anything that catches its eye and claws at anything that moves—it brings terror and decay until its eyes are drawn elsewhere. The village leaders have fallen away, and war councils have taken their place. These councils put their everything into fighting against the beast. They burn crops, slaughter livestock, and urge every carpenter and smith into building defenses. They spend years constructing walls and barricades. Every child is raised to hold a pitchfork to defend from the creature. Schools rot on the edge of towns and bell towers crumble in disrepair. There is no dreaming, no invention within the forest's reach. It is a lifetime of preparing for an unkillable foe. It is a lifetime dreading the return of a monster with no agenda—a monster who may never appear again, but of course, always does.

Cradle

Before The Wilting Rose perceived Her monsters, She felt the death they brought. She felt Her beloved mortals being robbed of fleeting life—being stolen by claws and flames and the sea—being dragged away into The Land of the Dead. Grief gnawed at Her heart. The Goddess lamented the rising tide of death. She clutched Her hands to Her aching chest and made a single wish: A wish to slow the flow of souls away from the realm She liberated. A wish to keep Her people happy and thriving under the light of The High Heavens at any cost. Her wish seeped into the soil of The Mortal Realm. It reached out to dying things—to anything halfway between the Earth and The Land of the Dead. It seized trees rotted away by fungus and the bodies of animals mere inches away from being consumed as carrion. It dragged their innards below the Earth, leaving skin and bark on the surface. It gathered heartwood and sap. It gathered muscle, marrow, and bone. It gathered them beneath the soil, and brought them together into a body suiting The Goddess's wish

The result was a single massive hand. It had crooked fingers long enough to reach across continents. The fingers were made of rotten bending wood, but they had patches of crimson flesh spiraling across them. The flesh was adhesive and slimy, it was the consistency of congealed blood trickling down from fingertips to the entity's palm. Its palm looked like the sight of a massacre. It was a mountain of corpses flattened into a paste—a coat of deep red that closened its connection to death. It followed the escaping souls of every half-dead thing it had built itself from. It trailed them to the afterlife they hoped to escape to, and as it reached their destination, it closed its fingers around the gates. It sealed off The Land of the Dead. It refused to let even the trees that it had drawn into the Earth to pass from the world that its Goddess loved. From that moment on, any soul that slipped away from The Mortal Realm would not find itself in the world they were called to. Instead, they would find themselves caught within the fingers of The Wilting Rose's wish. Their spirits would crash against its adhesive flesh and add to the mass of the blockade.

The Goddess of Roses felt a burst of joy. Her hopes had come to pass. She could feel the flow of souls slowing—She could feel death stealing fewer and fewer of Her beloved mortals away. Even those that approached the entrance of the world beyond refused to move on. She could feel some lingering at its gates, surely hesitating before leaving their lives behind, surely feeling Her drawing them back for a second chance. Others had already begun to flee its pull. She could feel them gathering in graveyards and on battlefields. She could feel their spirits returning home. What She couldn't feel was the state of their souls. She'd been too relieved to realize that the spirits that fled to the surface were unable to reclaim their bodies, that they'd remained spirits. Life was not so easy to restore, even for the Queen of The High Heavens. She had prevented them from leaving The Mortal Realm, but She had granted them no release from death. The Wilting Rose had damned them—She'd created haunted patches of Earth where souls lacking vitality cowered from the gates of death.

The Wilting Rose would never know what Her wish had wrought. She would never again gaze upon The Land of the Dead and see Her fist closed upon it. She would go about Her days soaking up the feeling of souls gathering at the jaws of death, but not taking another step. She would let their presence lull Her into some approximation of comfort. She would be consoled by the knowledge that no matter what happened going forward, that no matter what corruption and decay threatened the world that She adored, She would not have to face it alone. Until the destruction of realms above and below, She would have company. She would never have to wish for someone to suffer alongside.

Portrait of a Mad Goddess

In the deep hours of the night, on days when even The Wilting Rose rests and Her eyes close on the worlds below Her, a devil appears in The Realm of Mortals. A devil whose visage has been described to me in every tavern I've stopped in. They tell of a creature whose face is locked in a tortured scowl—with features framed by sculpted wrinkles—lines as hard as stone that hold her face in a state of endless rage. She always bares her teeth—sharp like fangs, but with none of the uniform grace of a wandering beast. Instead her jaw is filled with jagged stones, like those at the edge of a seaside cliff; blood dripping to her chin as they grind against one another like waves in an endless storm. Her skin, pulled tight against her bones, is the faded pink of a dying flower—a detail that's never missed. Nearly every inch of her is on display through the tatters of what must have been a dress and the oily hair stuck to her skull. They say that despite her wretched state, she holds herself with pride. That she stands perfectly straight and walks with steady, swaying hips—that she's almost regal in posture as she heralds in oblivion.

The devil hunts for crowds—for caravans and crowded halls. Her nails drag against every door she passes. Her screams ring across the towns she visits. She doesn't kill a soul, until there's someone to watch her do the deed. But once she's gathered eyes, she begins to tear them out. She kills anyone within reach, then anyone who tries to stop her. Anyone who's seen her curtseying in the town center is sure to witness death. She carves a bloody path, sure to show her face to every passerby, sure to leave a description for surviving city guards and ghost stories told on moonless nights. The devil's rage has never lasted beyond a single evening. The massacre lasts as long as the sun is down, but her will to fight evaporates the moment that pink and orange flood the sky. When the day reveals itself, she flees from sight, evading all capture—seemingly vanishing into the morning mist.

It took months of hunting for me to find her. It was by providence alone that I was startled awake by the screams of a gathering crowd. I hurried from my bed, hardly taking the time to dress. I ducked through alleys and hopped the fence of the guardhouse. I muscled through the crowd until my eyes found her: the devil I'd dreamed of recording. She was exactly as they'd said, though they'd failed to capture one detail. When she moved, her body seemed to fade to mist. It was like watching watercolor drip across a canvas, like a perfect painted image strolling through the half-woken world. I watched in awe as she took trained soldiers apart with her hands alone. I followed, scribbling in my book as she chased bystanders fool enough to flee her. She made them look at her before she broke their necks—she made sure every wicked deed was perceived. It was like food to her, seeing people quake with terror, seeing people scan her face for any redeeming feature. I could feel her need, her need for eyes, her need to hear the word monster screamed in her direction. She found solace in it, pleasure, even. At least, until the sky showed signs of light.

Morning signaled its approach, and following every tale I'd heard, she ran. I was the only one who followed—the only one who needed to see where she would go. Soldiers beckoned for me to stop, to cut my losses and to flee with the rest, but I refused. I had no family to avenge, no home to protect. All I had was curiosity and a book full of beasts that begged for company. I ran until I could no longer find a trail of trickling blood—until her presence no longer screamed to me through the walls. She'd vanished in an alley with no exit—slipped from my grasp without anywhere to run to. I scanned the roofs, the trees, even the sky itself for any sign of the devil, but no satisfaction found me. None, at least, until my eyes drifted to The High Heavens. There, I saw her limping past the gates. She stumbled forward, losing mass with every inch, until she reached the palace's inner chambers. There, I watched her approach the sleeping body of The Wilting Rose.

I saw her climb into the skull of The Goddess and disappear. Only then did The Goddess wake as if jolted by a nightmare. She raised Her arms to inspect Her skin. She felt Her teeth and hair. She smoothed Her skirt, checking it for tears, and rose to Her feet. She stumbled through Her palace until She found a mirror and continued to inspect Herself. For a moment, the devil appeared. For a moment, The Wilting Rose saw her. Or maybe, She only saw Herself the way everyone sees Her in The Realm of Mortals: a wicked beast who brought war and death, who tore a hole in the world She couldn't find a way to fix. The fear of their hate, of them seeing such a ghastly thing where She stood, brought resentment to the front of Her mind. If this was how they truly saw Her, it almost made Her

wish… no, those thoughts were best left for the
lonesome hours of the night—for nightmares
She could never share.

Cathedral

As a reward to Her most beloved followers, The Wilting Rose made a house of worship. The hilltop cathedral was to be Her greatest creation in The Mortal Realm. She showered the hillside with seeds until it was covered in a sea of roses. The stone leading to the cathedral was reshaped into a natural stairway, an invitation from the Heavens themselves. Next, she raised the building from the Earth and bid it to shape itself into a church as tall as a castle. Trees twisted through the windows until they'd transformed into rafters and pillars. The Goddess of Roses delicately applied a rose-tinted gold to the trim of the building and to the rosewood pews She placed across the floor. From the planet's center, She drew reserves of iron and forged a set of awe inspiring double doors with floral patterns weaved into every inch. She gave every stained glass window a piece of Her legacy: the invention of roses, festivals shared between nymphs and mortals, the dethroning of the gods, and the divine gifts She offered to humans in the aftermath—the allowance for them to rebuild on their own terms and seize their own arcane destiny.

She agonized over every detail. There had to be a hundred pews, enough to hold whatever host of followers Her chosen guides would bring here. The walls had to be lined with portraits of the witches and generals who'd answered Her rallying cry against the gods. And of course, at the building's head, there had to be an altar. She placed a simple wooden shrine down to face the pews. Any further decor would be the choice of Her worshipers. Her worship, and the ceremonies that She had earned would be in their hands. After all, where would She be without them? How would She have taken heaven's throne without the aid of the humans who loved Her? She thought only of their embrace, and the songs of praise She was unsure She deserved as She constructed the temple of Her dreams.

Even in as gentle and deliberate a creation as this, The Wilting Rose was incapable of keeping the ruin within Her at bay. As She stocked the altar with ritual wine, something spilled from Her. Just a drop of resentment, of distrust—one question to which She couldn't fathom an answer. Nothing noticeable, and yet, enough to shatter worlds. The drop was soaked into the foundation. That tear of doubt became a single

flaw in the stone, a hole beneath the altar, was
all that it took for the cathedral to drink of Her
doubts—doubts that solidified within its design
and spread into newly formed cracks. She led a
selection of Her followers up the hill. They
made the trek up the stone steps, past the sound
of thorny brambles shifting beneath their feet.
Roses turned to behold the worshipers as they
approached, but could only greet them with
browning petals and the incense of decay. They
pressed beyond every concern and slipped
through the double doors that opened just long
enough for each body to slip through before
sealing themselves again.

As they beheld their Goddess's designs, they
tried with all their might to ignore the flaws. The
wooden pillars groaned as patches of rot
threatened to bring them down. The floor had
spiraling cracks running across it. Perhaps most
concerning, the wooden altar at the room's head
was barely visible—it had been overrun by a
cage of bramble from the field. As the eager
worshipers of The Goddess approached the altar,
the cathedral burst to life. The ground split
beneath them and their legs were seized by
thorny vines. The vines drew them down to their
knees in prayer. The room's wooden structures

groaned again, a deep, elongated cry of one impossible question: Why?

Why did they worship Her? Why did they love Her even as She let their world turn to rot? Why would they mock Her with songs of praise? That question had spilled from Her, and as Her followers sat helpless, unable to answer, they were punished. Their legs were shredded by thorns. Their skin was burned by radiant light as stained glass images scowled with resentment. The stone shot up to their arms and dragged their hands down into a bow, then crushed their wrists for complying. The vines delivered libation wine to each of the cathedral's prisoners and doused them with it until the altar was empty. Some of them drowned in ritual liquid. Others fell as their eyes were burned by the pale pink light searing through the windows. Those who endured wine and light and blood loss could only watch as the most outspokenly devout among them faded from the world.

The survivors were forced to hold their kneeling bows as their punishment continued. They were tortured until one of them managed to scream out—to condemn The Wilting Rose and curse Her as an enemy. The cathedral fell silent. Finally, they revealed themselves. Traitors, charlatans, enemies who jeered and mocked the church and spit at its creator. Now that they had confessed the motive of their worship, they could be dealt with. Her enemies were freed of bramble, wine, and blinding light as the cathedral reset itself. They were offered a moment of breath, a moment to thank no one in particular that they'd been freed. The cracks beneath them began to worsen. The floor split and swallowed every kneeling follower of The Wilting Rose. The spiraling cracks in the cathedral floor were stained crimson—the only sign that someone had once worshiped here. With time, the cathedral repaired itself. It hid enough of the gore and cracks to seem presentable from the hill's base. It did its best to make itself seem shiny and new—to draw in another flock to kneel at its altar. A flock whom it could ask the same question and push until it found an honest answer.

The Indulgent Cult

Not every drop of The Wilting Rose's Essence found its way into a monster. Some expressions of misery lacked the coherence to take shape. Her sobs have infected rivers and food stores, they've given towns a sweeping wave of Her suffering without warning. Her screams have created an air of hostility overnight—a feeling of tension that grips tight enough to ruin lives. These instances were unremarkable, the plights of the gods have long found their way into the hearts of humans. But as Her essence came in larger waves, some began to notice its arrival. In an otherwise unremarkable town, one free of monsters, plague, and war, The Goddess' corrupting bile found its way into a bottle. It was captured by the mayor, who told the head of the farming guild, who told the poet whom she had eyes for, who told her highest paying patron. They gathered to discuss the bile, to observe it, to taste it.

One among them thought to touch the substance to their tongue. They let it sit within their mouth, to let it burn away their taste buds with the taste of citrus past its date. The moment they swallowed, the essence overtook them. They were overwhelmed by Her sadness, Her rage, Her isolation. They gained knowledge of The High Heavens: how it felt to die, the ways humanity may crumble, the sensation of a thousand awful things crawling across the Earth—knowing that one was responsible for every tragedy they caused. The sensation, as they described it, was like having the sea forced through their ears. It was like The Goddess's own thoughts flooded their brain, like every instance of human suffering crawled beneath their skin as a swarm of maggots. Enthralled by this description, they were each compelled to take a taste. They each described it differently. They argued over the ways it tore their minds apart, the ways that misery entered them like never before—like an experienced lover leaving them unable to walk.

They agreed to keep the experience a secret. Its taste was theirs alone. They parted ways, but could not forget the feeling. It visited them in dreams, it bled into their personal lives and their poetry. Their worlds were painted by thick gray blots. In less than a month they gathered again to experience it. They locked themselves in the mayor's estate and drained the bottle dry. They felt the talons of beasts tearing through peasantry, they mimicked the wails of spirits left to wander, they soaked in despair and cackled with glee. In their week of isolation they painted the countryside rotting away and sang to the tune of Her cries. They ate as if they'd been starved and fucked with a desperation that they had never felt before. Their own misery only settled in when the bottle ran dry. Her essence was finite, and they were left without inspiration.

It was then that they sealed their pact: those who had gathered to drink of Her bile agreed to travel the world. They would go anywhere a trace of Her essence could be felt and take it for themselves. They would travel to villages ravaged by monsters, and they would bottle any pieces of still-living tragedy they could find. The drops they collected would feed the mayor's vineyard, and every time new grapes grew, they would join together again. How else would they be inspired to love and to capture the world for what it was? What was the purpose of disaster if not to find the thunderous harmonies within? They were blessed with insight into the suffering of humankind, and on their watch, it would not go to waste.

Confession

I fear that I've created an evil all my own—that in recording these aberrations, I have taken a piece of each of them and pressed them deep into the page—that if we could slay every monster that plagues us, they would simply slip out of my book, and start the madness all over again. When my eyes scan the pages, I feel the weight of every word building in my stomach. That feeling rises through my chest and fills me to the top of my throat. I feel too heavy to move, too full to eat, too weighed down by the evil I've committed. When I touch quill to paper, my arms begin to itch as if two serpents have burrowed under my skin—finding space between my muscles to coil around my bones. They tighten themselves around me and lock my wrists down to the page. They compel me to write beyond what I could possibly know—to record every evil that passes from The High Heavens to the unworthy dirt beneath my feet. When I flip through the pages of my catalog of abominations; I can hear it whispering to me. It tells me the truth of my crimes. It tells me every way that I have failed my fellow humans, and the way that I have undone my Goddess by recording Her shame. It would be enough to drive one over the edge, though I fear true madness could never take one gifted by divine sight as I have been.

Oh, Wilting Rose. Oh, Goddess who rules The High Heavens. If you can read this, I beg you to strike me down. I wear my sins openly—I refuse to conceal the crimes I have committed against you. If your eyes have fallen upon the pages of my catalog of abominations on this land and you despise me for them, then I readily accept my punishment. I am prepared to fall into the deepest pits of death, beyond the realms which you have barred us from entering, while my legacy burns. If you see fit to place your hand upon this world again, let it be to crush my throat. Even knowing that my work is abhorrent I cannot stop. I have become a conduit for your misery, and I don't know what I would be without it. My life is evil and unworthy of your hand, but I cannot bring myself to oblivion. I cannot. I cannot. I must keep writing. The beasts of this world must be given shape… Their sins must be carried within me—within stories and songs that pour from my wretched hands.

Why has my Goddess forsaken me twice?
Does She not see me?

Does She not see the beasts that rampage across
Her world?
Does She hate me this much?
Why was I gifted the rose?
It traveled all this way
Just to take my mind.
There must have been a reason
I must have been chosen by Her—
Chosen to carry this world's end,
Chosen to carry the burden of what
Only She and I can truly know.
I cannot stop recording them
I cannot stop seeking them out
I cannot stop
I cannot stop
She won't let me stop.
Perhaps this is my hell:
My punishment for the sins
She knew I would fall into,
Perhaps the temptation of the parasite
That now rots my mind, was the sin
That I was always guilty of
And now in atonement
I must carry its weight
For as long as humanity carries on.
I accept this burden, my Goddess,
I thank you for your eyes on me.
I thank you for this absolution
For this taste of holy hell.

The Garden of the Nymphs

Rejoice, oh nymphs, for the gods are dead! The cause for which your Sister rallied you to fight and die has been concluded. Never again must you soil your delicate hands with the blood of the divine. Never again must you strain yourselves to the point of breaking to save your realm, and every other. So begin your century long celebration, oh nymphs! Drown yourselves in wine and lose yourselves to dance and lovemaking. Forget the trials of decades that now come to an end. Forget The High Heavens where your Sister now lives. Where She longs for company, for someone to help Her hold the burden of all creation—a burden no true nymph would ever think to hold. Surely your Sister, lost to you when She took the throne, is happier now than when She was a silent rose tending to Her section of the garden, without so much as a smile. Surely She is satisfied with the role that you played and bids you now to rest. You pledged yourselves to fight—you pledged yourselves to justice—and justice has been served. What's left to do? What cause is left to rally to, besides to nurse the wounds of war and

let them be forgotten—let them fade into song
and legend?

You never hear Her cries of agony. They are
drowned out by the screams of empty praise that
you offer to Her at your banquet's beginning.
You do not feel Her begin to wilt for you've
inhaled the smoke of Seer's Sage and your
minds have wandered to visions of the paradise
that She dreamed to create for you, and every
mortal that you haven't noticed begging for
relief from famine, war, and monsters born of
Her despair. You never notice, decades down the
line, Her last attempt to connect with Her sisters.
Her last return to the garden that She can no
longer enter. You've let your plants indulge in
the cups of your enchanted wine and they've
grown so thick and unwieldy that not even you
can prune them back—not even you can
navigate your gardens, or reach the realms
beyond. It will be centuries before your minds
return to you. It will be centuries before you
ponder the state of the world, less liberated from
responsibility. It will be centuries too late when
you finally grow tired of feast, of songs, of
Seer's Sage, and the taste between the legs of
your fellow nymphs. When you finally see the
rot that has taken The Mortal Realm and the
devastation that has taken your Divine Sister.

Will you care, then? Or will you be too busy
tending to your overgrown garden? Will you be
too busy planning the next party to celebrate the
day that someone comes to your door and rallies
you to slay the monsters that your Sister made
and the monster that you let Her become.

Her Most Faithful

Her most faithful knew that their war was a just and righteous one. They knew mortals needed champions—that they longed for noble souls to serve their needs with fire and fury. They begged Her for power. They battled the gods and shook the gates of The High Heavens. They stood with knights and peasants, and seized the destiny of their world in human hands.

Her most faithful were all too eager to slay the priests of the gods of old. Those who hoarded magic for themselves and turned their eyes from those who needed them. These priests let peasants starve and cities burn if it meant they'd keep the favor of the gods—gods who cared little for lives in The Realm of Mortals, so long as they had prayers to feast upon. These priests were tyrants, and as wicked as the divinity they served. It was a noble thing to strike them down, to sever their fingers and carve out their tongues. To strip them of the holy symbols they used to warp the world and throw them on a pyre.

Her most faithful swore to nurture the Earth. To let humanity heal from the wrath of holy war.

Once again flowers would flourish in blood soaked soil. Magic would soar in the heart of every mortal. They swore that the strife of the Heavens would never again bring humanity to its knees. They crumbled the temples of the old gods. They buried the memory of the tyrant pantheon and built churches in Her image—churches with rose crests and brilliant gardens—churches where all could behold the ones who had freed them. The Goddess of Roses and her loyal champions, the first riders into the age of the mortal. They built churches where one could find celebration and song. They shared Her words—her appreciation of simple and beautiful things. They told anyone who would listen of the value of the human heart in her kingdom, and of human creations in her eyes.

Her most faithful graciously settled on the thrones of banished kings. After all, someone had to rule. Someone had to look after the peasantry and guide Her knights in holy quests. It was their burden to interpret the words of the new queen of The High Heavens—their sacred duty to hold feasts in their own honor. Who else could perform Her will? Who else could fathom Her needs, besides her first and most faithful followers?

Her most faithful wore the emblems of the old gods. They kept everything they found on the priests of the former faith. They channeled what power they could from the rotting gods they deposed. They wear their charms beneath their vestments. They hide them in the altars on which they promised to live and die by Her hope; all while mimicking the motions of severed fingers and the forbidden words of tongues they cut out.

Her most faithful still held the power She gave them with open arms. They still perform rites and rituals in Her name. Never once, while indulging in the essence of Her enemies, did they turn their backs on Her gifts—gifts they claim are theirs alone. Rewards for loyalty and valor, that no other could wield with such purpose. They clutch to their chests the spells She wished to see in the hands of every mortal. The power that She surrendered so that there would never again be war over Heaven's plans for The Realm of Mortals.

Her most faithful drove out the witches: The Rosebud Coven, who served Her long before war—who loved Her long before She'd left the arms of the nymphs. The Rosebud Coven, who performed miracles of healing, and asked for nothing in return. They drove out these peddlers of spells, who never understood Her true intentions. Who always questioned the insight She'd given to Her favorite priests. They ignored Her cries as they speared Her favorite mortals. They stripped the rank of any knight who shielded their faces from stones. All in the name of their beloved Goddess of Roses, they purged any who twisted the words they delivered from The High Heavens.

Her most faithful were damned in Her eyes. Her priests walked with curses upon them from up high. Their cities were overcome with plague and besieged by monsters bearing roses. She sent oblivion to tear them apart, to level any city rebuilt by their hands. She wanted their thrones burnt and their names forgotten. She wanted them to beg for mercy so She could deny them as they had Her will.

Her most faithful stood unbothered. They carried their curses in the charms of old gods and the hands of old priests. They wrote papers of the sins that brought plagues, and the disobedience that summoned beasts. Beloved priests gave sermons on the piercing screams from Heaven: what they meant, and how to tune them out. With every explanation they drew their people closer to their light—to Her light. No matter

what hell fell upon their churches, Her most
faithful spoke in Her name. Her will was theirs,
even as She begged them to stand aside.

Her most faithful cheered when The Goddess of
Roses began to wilt—when She let Her essence
become poison and The High Heavens Her
tomb. They toasted and drank as they became
the only ones to wield Her words. As their
Goddess grew weak and weary, they would be
the only ones to hold the vision of a righteous
world. They would be the only ones to command
the powers of Heaven, which had become their
own.

Conjoined

There were some who still prayed to the gods of old: nobles who had been torn from their seats when The Wilting Rose ascended, champions who had been banished and left to wander the wastes at society's edge, peasants, merchants, and artisans whose lives had not changed as much as promised—who still found comfort in the old emblems when the world still turned in the same direction. In return for their silent piety, these followers of fallen gods were gifted visions. In dreams, they were beckoned away to a kingdom in the far mountains. They were promised salvation if only they would leave their lives behind. Overnight, homes and stores were abandoned. Earthly possessions were burned while their owners slipped away. Kings, warriors, and servants of the old faith gathered together to make the treacherous trip and find what they'd been promised—to grasp at any hope of reclaiming The High Heavens.

They found their reward in a ruined kingdom at the mountain range's center. They were greeted by a collapsing citadel and a collection of hovels within its walls. In the citadel's inner sanctum sat two gods: the twin patrons of war. The elder twin looked as perfect as the day he'd emerged in the world. He had flowing raven hair, his skin was pristine and fair, his long, delicate fingers gripped a spear from the armory of The High Heavens. Next to him sat the younger twin, dressed in the full regalia of a war god. He wore shining silver armor and a cloak of starlight. He was rare among the gods, for he had never hidden the scars that lined his body. He wore each wound with the pride of one who had endured the worst of every war—one who had survived demons, monsters, and even divinity's overthrow with a bloody ax in hand. Only their top halves could be seen, their bodies had sunk into the castle's floor. Even still, they towered over those who had gathered before them.

The twin gods offered their followers an opportunity; they gave them the chance to serve divinity again. If they would make this citadel their home and pledge their lives to the cause of war, the gods would grow to claim The High Heavens. They swore on their still-beating hearts that they would rise to the challenge if only they had a kingdom worthy of claiming as their holy capital on Earth. The worshipers fell to their knees. They were overwhelmed by the sight of two gods in near perfect condition, of the chance to reclaim the lives they'd lost. The nobles were the first to rise, to pledge themselves to rule the world again. They settled into the crumbling towers atop the citadel to watch over the kingdom's progress. The champions rose next, swearing their swords to the cause of destroying The Goddess of Roses. They cleared the kingdom of beasts, and urged peasants to work the soil so life could grow again. The artisans sprang to action—they began what work they could to keep the castle from collapsing. Peasants and merchants settled into broken hovels. They happily settled in ruined homes, placing holy emblems over holes in the walls.

When their newfound kingdom reached its peak—when servants filled their crumbling hall, the twin gods posed a query to their followers. When they performed the inevitable feat of retaking The High Heavens—when The Wilting Rose had been slain and her skull split open to let divinity flow free: which of them should have the larger piece? Which brother deserved to sit atop Heaven's throne while the other served as its soldier? The elder brother, the god of strategy—of swift and silent war—boasted a quiet return to the ways of old. He would raise the gods whose bodies rotted shallow graves among the stars, and give them new life in his perfect pantheon. He would grant the nobles of old their land, he would allow them a peaceful walk back into grace. The younger brother, the god of battle and glory, of a war that ends in screams, promised much the opposite. He would burn the world to ash, and make a new one in his image. Those that fought beside him would be the founders of a new age of pride and steel. It would be instant, bloody, and offer the warriors who fought in his name a chance to reclaim their realm with swords in hand.

Their followers could not agree. They argued for their favorite plan with a fire not felt in their chests since the gods had died. In mere minutes, factions were born. In minutes, the citadel erupted into war. Nobles rallied champions, champions rallied peasants, and peasants' bodies began to line the halls. The gods urged their followers on: the elder snaked through the stone floor as far as he could, thrusting his spear towards his brother. The younger, not to be bested, hurled axes and daggers towards his sibling, forcing a retreat to the back wall. The struggle between the gods tore fissures in the castle floor. Injured soldiers tumbled through the cracks into the ruined undercroft. The zealous warriors of the brothers of war paid no mind to falling rubble and crumpling corpses. They pressed on, determined to prove their god the more worthy of the two. They swore the final hours of their broken lives to the fight. Any cost was worth restoring Heaven.

The brothers marveled at the ferocity of their followers. They praised them for their dedication, and silently mocked them for their stupidity. In all their joy at seeing two gods alive again, and all their dedication to killing in their name, they'd failed to notice the lingering wounds of the twin deities. The delicate hands of the elder twin had been flayed—leaving only long fractured finger bones. His flowing hair only barely concealed the eye that had been plucked from his skull. His skin, always fair, now lacked signs of blood. The younger of the two had hardly even attempted to conceal the holes in his armor where swords and thorns had torn him apart: entrails leaked from his breastplate, he always had a hand covering gashes in his throat. The brothers had been killed along with the rest. They'd found a way to elongate their existences beyond oblivion, a desperate method of survival to keep their corpses moving. But their followers had failed to see it. Never once had they looked down as the floor crumbled. None of them would ever see what had become of the brothers' lower halves.

The way that they'd melted into one, undead god.

Below their torsos sat a bloody slime that tethered them to life, and to each other. As the floor gave way to the castle's lower chambers, as bodies slipped below the surface, the congealed wound expanded. It fed upon the corpses of their loyal subjects and fed the gods the shredded souls. Every worshiper's death was a piece of them sustained. The soul of a champion could keep their skin from rotting any further. The bodies of a hundred peasants would allow them to stand tall, to rise further as the sludge that kept them moving was filled with life. But the warriors of the twins would never notice. They would fight and die for their vision of Heaven, for the conquest of a god that would never rise that high again.

Sirens

The Equinox had come again—faster than She'd
hoped. The calendar had begun to take laps
around the head of The Wilting Rose. Weeks
were born and died in the time it took Her to
breathe. Years fell away in the time it took Her
to mourn the loss of the weeks. The dreaded day
had come. The sun burst to life to chase away
the frost of winter. The stars pulled back to make
the passage clear. On this day, lines between The
High Heavens and The Realm of Mortals grew
impossibly thin. And from the highest peak of
the oldest mountain, Pilgrims could see past the
gates of Heaven. Their eyes could wander into
the palace and behold their beloved Queen:
naked and wallowing, in a puddle of filth and
misery.

She'd needed time to prepare—to dress
Herself—to make Herself their Goddess again.
But it was far too late. The day neared its peak,
and Her followers had braved the mountain. She
could hear their footsteps echoing towards Her
chambers. She could all but feel their laughter
caressing Her ear: the joy, the hope of seeing a
grand display, the chance to bow before Her

Majesty. As The Wilting Rose felt worshipers near, Her body began to boil. A furnace erupted in Her chest as the heat of shame awoke. It threatened to boil Her heart to grease. Her arms felt weak as the fire curled up to burst against Her cheeks. Her faded pink flesh grew red as She pictured them looking upon Her. As She pictured disappointment on their faces and the shame of it all burnt Her away. It was all too much: the heat, the sound of footsteps nearing the peak, the whole accursed Equinox. She had to banish it—to make it quiet—to cool Her aching flesh.

And so, The Wilting Rose banished Her shame. She let it flare from Her body, and drift onto the mountain: formless, nameless, out of Her sight. Its heat was caught in the wind—it was drawn to the mountain. It slipped past the pilgrims and into a crack in the rocky face of the mountain on which they settled.

One of the devout perceived Her voice in the blistering wind that raced past their ears. This way, it beckoned, Find me, See me, Let me take you in my embrace. The pilgrim led her party down, into the curving caverns, far from the peak, and the face of their withering queen. Beneath the mountain sat a labyrinth, stone carved by time into an endless twisting path. The air grew thick with heat, heat that felt like swallowing steel. The heat made the cavern walls hotter than a potter's kiln. It filled the vision of the eager pilgrims with dancing waves—waves that had captured The Goddess's shame. Her shame took shape in distorted air: the shape of a body much like Her own. Her worshipers saw flashes of flowing hair and slender legs. Her worshipers saw the shape of their regal queen, of the ruler of their dreams, of the one who had urged them below the peak.

The image was incomplete, mere flashes of the one they'd dreamed to meet. But it was enough—enough to send them sprinting forward—enough for them to follow the flash of a body into the depths of the maze. Even as the shape split into three, six, nine visions of The Wilting Rose they wouldn't be deterred. The frantic followers of the elusive Goddess let their traveling band splinter. They were each drawn away, until they'd forgotten their friends, and the only sight they could still make out was the briefest glimpse of their Goddess urging them on. Further and further down through the winding labyrinth that would be their home. The shame of The Wilting Rose delayed the travelers until the Equinox ended. It compelled them to

run beyond exhaustion: until the sun had settled
again, the stars had fallen back in line, and the
realms stretched far apart.

Yet the embarrassment that had borrowed Her
image could find no rest. The pilgrims would not
be denied. They cared little for getting lost. They
cared little for food or rest. They cared only for
their Goddess and for the chance to look upon
Her face. The sensation of their eyes scanning
for Her in every flash of its bodies, and the
feeling of their hands grasping at its waves, kept
the shame burning bright. Their desire kept it
from falling away. It was forced to run further
and deeper—forced to flee down any path they
hadn't reached. The followers would not cease.
They ran towards the heat—the sensation of
divinity caressing their faces and whispering
through the wind. They ran even as their legs
split open and shreds of bloody skin gave way.
They propped themselves on searing stones.
They pushed themselves forward from the walls,
even as their hands boiled into nothing. They ran
beyond pain, beyond fear, beyond even where
death should have taken them. They looked
forever forward; their eyes melted into their
sockets, keeping them from looking beyond their
path.

According to rumors, the pilgrims still chase their quarry. If one travels to the oldest mountain, where the Equinox reveals the Heavens, they can hear the echoing stomps of skeletal feet. One can feel the rush of wind, always only one step ahead of them—unable to dissipate, to die, or to satisfy the undying who long for a face it doesn't have.

Euthanasia

The Wilting Rose dragged Her creation to the executioner's block. She stumbled back as the ax rose above her and its full weight reached Her shoulders. It had been a difficult decision, but this creature had to be destroyed. It had been Her last attempt to make something—to create one beautiful piece of life and prove that She had a vision and purpose enough to stand before The Mortal Realm. The Wilting Rose had a host of half-formed ideas for Her greatest creation: worms made of thorny brambles to scatter across the Earth, a colossal canine to guard the paths between realms, or perhaps a brilliant bird of prey—one that could capture starlight on moonless nights. Conflicting images clouded Her vision. She struggled to think of anything but the act of creation itself. Her mind wandered to the joy of a completed work, but She couldn't picture the details, only a blurred image of a brilliant beast of the Heavens. Each potential creature battled for supremacy within Her mind. They begged for lives that She couldn't quite picture, screaming in voices that She could hardly make out. She forced Herself through the clouds to make something, anything, that could inspire awe.

The creature came to life for only an instant. Its body was that of a stillborn bird: pink, featherless, and crumpled. Beneath it sat the feathers of a full grown vulture, they spiraled around it in the shape of a pressed flower. Its head—heads—were those of undead dogs. Two massive canine skulls with dripping eyes looked up at The Wilting Rose expectantly. She recoiled and left them to pick away at the avian body they were fused to—at the spiny insects stuck below its skin. The creature had died the moment it was born. Its feathers flailed for less than a second. Even the worms within it had failed to burrow to safety before losing their life force. Only the heads of dogs still moved. They tried to drag their body towards their Goddess, towards the author of their untimely birth.

The Wilting Rose wanted to cry as She brought the ax down upon the canine heads of Her creation, but not a single tear shed for the creature as its twin skulls rolled into the dirt. The Goddess wrenched the stillborn bird from its mountain of feathers. She made a small incision in its malformed flesh to pluck the first of the bramble worms free, but when it pricked

Her finger, She flew into a rage. She sliced the creature in Her hand to pieces and ripped free each worm that She'd been stupid enough to grant spines. Her final deliberate creation sat before Her in four segments: the feathers crushed into Her symbol, the undead dog heads flailing purposelessly on the ground, the pile of blood covered bramble that had lived for only a moment, and the lump of useless pink flesh that She'd carved apart. This was Her legacy, these were the inspired creations that came from Her trembling hands.

The Goddess had planned to bury them—She'd already dug four holes beneath Her shriveled garden, but as She beheld the mess before Her, the attempt to bury Her shame seemed too good for Her. Instead, She gathered four pedestals from the abandoned temples of the gods and placed them around Her garden. Each piece of the beast She'd dreamed up was placed upon a marble plinth so that She would have to see it every time She dared leave Her palace, and so that anyone who dared approach Her desolate realm would know the reward of holding Heaven in one's hand.

Fit for a Queen

The coronation gown of The Goddess of Roses had only been worn on one occasion. It was the last time She was seen before a crowd—the last celebration before the gates of The High Heavens were sealed with their queen inside. The Goddess of Roses sauntered across the lines between realms. She gripped the rose red tulle of Her dress between gloved fingers. She was cloaked from elbow to fingertip in the same rose red as Her gown. With gold rings on each of Her fingers, and a wreath of the same glittering metal clasped around Her neck. On that night, The newly crowned Goddess descended. She moved with a host of nymphs drunk on battle and booze to The Mortal Realm they so adored. She claimed victory over the gods while sparkling like a treasury. Her garb was opulent, but so was the occasion, and She wasn't alone. Nymphs and humans retrieved their most brilliant robes and gowns to join Her in celebration. They were free, they were victorious, and they planned to drink away the memories of war. They danced from The Mortal Realm, through The Garden of Nymphs, to the gates of The High Heavens.

Together, they beheld the first sun of a new era, with every witness adorned in jewels.

She'd felt happy in those fleeting jovial moments. She'd felt worthy in the waves of cheering soldiers who'd bled for Her rebellion. She'd felt beautiful for one perfect instant as She saw reflections of Her coronation garb in passing. It was these memories that compelled The Wilting Rose to retrieve the gown from Her dressing room a second time. She slid on the puffy sleeves, layered like rose petals the same as Her skirt. Her legs slipped through the layers of tulle, but She froze before She finished. The bodice, with pink flowers sewn in every place She'd received a scar, sagged untightened from Her chest. The jewelry sat across from Her, unpolished and gathering dust. She beheld Herself in the mirror—She saw a faded thing with matted hair and sunken eyes stepping into a Goddess's gown. The sight of this wretched being in such stunning attire made The Wilting Rose release a long, pained laugh. Ugly, lowly, unworthy. Those were the things She saw, the features She fixated on as She scowled at Her reflection. She repeated the words over and over as She tossed the dress aside. Ugly, lowly, unworthy, She muttered to Herself as She stumbled from the chamber—as She fled to any room without a mirror.

The coronation gown of The Goddess of Roses never hit the ground. The dress remembered the weight of The Wilting Rose's body—the feeling of holding the queen who ruled in the Heavens and upon the Earth. It forced itself to stand, the same way She'd stood when She'd worn the dress with pride. Unworthy, that was the curse The Goddess had uttered underneath Her breath: She must have meant the dress. She must have deemed it unworthy of Her perfect body. The gown would have to prove itself, to show Her that it could rise to the occasion. That it could make itself worthy of adorning divinity. It gathered its gloves and jewels, it drew a blade from Heaven's armory. It marched, with a pair of The Goddess's heels for its feet, to The Realm of Mortals—to a place its owner loved. It marched with purpose, and a plan to prove that it could stand worthy of adorning divinity.

The Dress fought with the rage of a rebellious nymph and the might of an ascended god. The memory of Her waltz and Her drunken sprint was enough—just that fragment of The Goddess of Roses could inspire a massacre. It tore through armor with a flick of its glove. Its skirt flared as it twirled across fields of battle. Sellswords and bandits fell without so much as a tear in its delicate folds. With each life carved away, the gown sought greater challenge. It fought harder and louder. It would kill until The Wilting Rose noticed and deemed it worthy. The gown would not rest until its owner dragged it back to Her dressing room to wear it once again.

Word swept across the world of a specter dressed in rose red who had slain a hundred and never grown weary or weak. These stories reached the ears of the faithful Knights of the Rose. Some were skeptical, others were eager to prove the rumors wrong, and to banish this ghost in the name of their Goddess. Knights gathered by the hundreds and swept across the countryside until they saw a splash of red on the horizon. They charged against the gown with all their might: swords passed through its empty neckline, soldiers lost their footing as they failed to keep up with the dancing dress. Ten died in the first minute of the struggle—ten died before someone recognized the dress. As she studied the gown, one of the oldest of the knights felt a memory rushing to the forefront of her mind: a memory of a nymph who she'd bled beside for years, and the day that she'd danced with Her when the war had been won. The dress spun just

as the nymph had in the garden. Its steps were
exact as were the swings of its sword. It had to
be Her: The Goddess of Roses. The knight fell
to her knees.

The Knights of the Rose, believing themselves
in the presence of divinity, laid down their
blades. They pledged themselves to the service
of this dress—of the beloved Goddess who had
revealed Herself to them. Questions of why they
couldn't see Her were hushed. They were
unworthy to behold Her, they'd have to prove
themselves worthy of seeing the spark in Her
eyes or the delicate steps of Her feet. Each
knight swore their lives to the cause of the
gown. They would fight for it, die for it, follow
it into death with pride. The gown led its newly
acquired knights into war: they struck down the
last demons that walked freely upon the Earth,
they purged disloyal nobles who held onto their
armies, they marched on distant kingdoms. The
Knights of the Rose fought, killed, and died for
one desperate look at their chosen divinity. They
wandered the length of the world, slaying any
who denied the name of The Goddess. The dress
dragged them forward with endless ambition. It
hardly allowed them rest. It was far too hungry,
too eager to earn the eye of its wearer. With each
city burnt, the gown looked longingly towards

the stars, hoping that The Goddess would see it
from atop Her throne. All the while, The Wilting
Rose sat in Her mirrorless, windowless chamber
and sobbed. She hadn't noticed the dress's
absence, She hadn't noticed the spilling of
blood. All She could think about was how She'd
felt trying on Her gown again, and how She
cursed the day She'd had it made.

Herald

The Wilting Rose was startled to attention when
a piercing sound blasted through Her chambers.
It was a thick, heavy sound full of energy and
thunder, but it rose into a high and whimsical
one. It was like the boom of a cannon
threatening to turn into a screech as its shot
soared into the air. The sudden assailing noise
struck Her as odd; there was not another soul
occupying The High Heavens. There was
nothing to fill Her palace with such a
disturbance—nothing to interrupt Her from Her
wallowing. She exited Her chambers and
searched for the noise's source. She followed its
erupting screams up the palace stairs, beyond the
throne room, and out into the streets of Her
empty kingdom. In the open air, She recognized
the sound. It was the blaring of a trumpet and
one she'd heard before. The same sound had
pierced the air to welcome Her to Heaven the
first time She'd entered it not as a servant, or as
a conqueror, but as a queen. She had followed it
to the throne room, and allowed its regal tones to
beckon Her into the seat that She'd earned with
blood.

Hearing it again filled Her with the same
emotions She'd felt that day. Her heart had been

heavy and Her stomach restless. She hadn't known if She'd deserved such fanfare, or if She'd had any right to sit atop the throne. It was uncomfortable, but the trumpet's sound was ceaseless until She followed its cue. After that day, She'd scoured the archives of The High Heavens for any stories of a phantom trumpet, of a messenger of Heaven who welcomed its new rulers; She came up short. But now, hearing it again, She was determined to find its source. She needed to know who had been with Her that day—who had bid Her to seize Her throne. She needed to know who else still occupied the realm She'd sealed Herself within.

She could practically hear footsteps thundering just one street ahead of Her. Somehow, this entity stayed one beat ahead of Her no matter how fast She ran, and somehow it did so without running out of breath. She imagined a creature crawling through alleyways on four legs. A creature with a dozen arms on its back, carrying a dozen trumpets for its dozen mouths. Every time its breath grew thin and one set of lips began to ache, it must have switched to a new trumpet. That must have been what plagued Her, that must have been what was forcing Her to sprint down blood-stained roads and under deteriorating temples. As She passed through the ruined Heavens, She was again accosted by memories. She remembered how it felt to walk down these streets and realize that the gods had truly fallen—that flowers could grow here again, and that Her sisters and Her beloved humans would be able to walk through the gates of The High Heavens without restriction. Reality was finally Hers—was finally theirs. That was perhaps the only lasting perk of Her ascension; even if She had failed to remake Her realm, it could always be rebuilt. Perhaps that was why She grew furious imagining this hulking trumpeter threatening to topple Her temples—the temples of the fallen gods. As it lumbered past, summoning thunder from its lungs.

The trail went cold and The Goddess found Herself in an empty alleyway, but She still heard the horn. It was close, it was practically surrounding Her. The sound pushed harder and harder against Her ears, as if it were raining down from the sky. The sky… Perhaps She had been wrong about what monster She faced. Perhaps there was something gliding along the roofs of Her realm: something with the legs of a frog and the wings of a bat. Its movements were silent, save for the horn that it blew. Yes, She could feel it in the wind. The song it played was

so obviously coming from above Her. She raced
to the nearest temple, climbed up its wall, and
sprinted along its marble arches in search of Her
foe. This creature was playing with Her. It
laughed at Her for caring. Why did She put so
much importance into this sound? Why did She
assume that it played for Her? She tore across
the rooftops, desperate to find it, to find out why
it mocked Her so. She moved to taller and taller
buildings, until She found Herself at the top of
Her palace. It was the highest point in The High
Heavens, from here, She could see everything;
yet, She still could not see Her loathsome
trumpeter.

As She climbed down from the edge of Her
palace, the world went silent. Was it over? Had
this been a fleeting aberration? A final haunting
from one of the realm's former rulers? The
Wilting Rose began to catch Her breath, and for
a moment, Her mind began to quiet. That quiet
lasted seconds, as the trumpet blared to life
again louder than ever. It hit Her with such force
that She was knocked off Her feet. This time, it
had come from the palace. She raced into the
throne room to confront Her newest, greatest
enemy, but still the room was empty. She
scanned every niche of Heaven's throne room,
until Her eyes fell upon its centerpiece. The

throne loomed large as another trumpet blast brought Her to Her knees. She could practically see the metal twisting, transforming from gold to brass. This had been it all along… It had lured Her to its seat all those years ago. It despised Her for how hard She'd worked to kill its former owner. It despised Her for how badly She'd wanted to sit upon it.

On the day The Wilting Rose had first sat in Heaven's throne, She had felt all the emotions She'd remembered: sickness, unworthiness, sorrow; but She'd been proud, too. Proud to be the victor of a war that threatened to destroy Her. Proud to have beings from every realm acknowledging Her as their savior. She was proud to be queen, to be the ruler of Heaven and every deity that would come… She had wanted this. Oh, how badly She had wanted this. It was the dream that had kept Her fighting for so many years, the dream of having the seat of power, of being able to finally make the world work as it should. And here She was, in shambles, sobbing before a throne that was meant to be Hers. Here She was, letting The High Heavens sit empty atop The Mortal Realm while humans suffered and died. Here She was, unable to track down a single wandering musician, unable to keep Her kingdom quiet for even a moment.

Matching Eyes

The reign of the great demons had finally reached its conclusion. For centuries, demonic raiding parties poured from The Abhorrent Realm to terrorize humanity. Humans begged the gods for aid, but the gods remained unmoved. Afterall, they had not created the demons. Those were the plague of humanity. Demons were born of human sin, they mimicked the images of their crimes, they took on traits of their greatest fears. This was the greatest trial of The Mortal Realm. Humanity's burden was to prove themselves better and stronger than their darkest urges, and so the gods would offer no release. For a time, humanity was overrun. Their kingdoms were conquered, their greatest warriors eaten, and their peasantry were conscripted to build endless statues in honor of their captors. The tide wasn't turned until a humble nymph revealed a secret. She whispered the truth into the ears of witches: the first demons had once been gods. It was their corruption that had birthed the first lords of The Abhorrent Realm and it was their sins that shaped those of mortals. The only reason that demons lived was to keep humans from reaching for the throne of Heaven.

When The Goddess of Roses seized The High Heavens, Her first act was a declaration of war against the Abhorrent Lords. She showed humanity the power the gods had always held as she struck down demons with hardly a thought. The Mortal Realm rallied behind The Goddess. Together, they drove their would-be conquerors back to their festering abyss. A force of heroes guarded every gate to The Abhorrent Realm. They waited for the order of their Goddess—for permission to kill the last wretched pawns of the old regime. But the war had been long, and the world had not been well. The last legs of the campaign against the demons had happened without Her knowledge. She had earned the name The Wilting Rose, and She had sealed Herself away before the final blow could be dealt. The knights that wore Her symbol waited, but they received no order, they were once again without relief from The High Heavens.

A last council of demons was gathered. Their kingdoms had crumbled. Their allies on the Earth and in The High Heavens had been destroyed. It was the final hour of The Abhorrent Realm. Alone, the last Abyssal Lords would be wiped from the face of this and every realm. Only together could they endure the blade of The Wilting Rose. Only with one united arm of unrivaled might could they forge a new empire on the bones of mortals. Every surviving demon offered their essence. They poured every wicked aspect of the fallen gods, every sin they'd found in the kings of men, and every wish to burn the realms that had spurned them into one, perfect body. The carcasses of the last Abyssal Lords fell limp, and from them rose a queen. The Last Demon had skin the pale gray of faded paint in water. Her body was roughly the shape of a human's; its surface looked ordinary and smooth at first glance. Only upon further study would one notice the faces swimming beneath the surface. The face of every Abyssal Lord that birthed the demon swam within her; they monitored their domain and whispered their desires to her. They commanded her to rise and topple the world so adored by The Goddess.

The Last Demon made no move to obey her creators. She simply sat atop the throne of The Abhorrent Realm, and waited. Her presence was felt by every hero camped along the mouths of her empty kingdom. They charged into the festering abyss to snuff out whatever light their foes had sought to brighten. The Last Demon made quick work of champions of The Wilting Rose. Their swords could not break her skin, their feet could not match her speed, their armor was useless against her fists, which crushed through steel and ribs with ease. The demon kept their bodies. She adorned them in the bones of her fallen kin and armed them with weapons of The Abhorrent Realm. The only pieces of them she left exposed were the emblems of roses. Anything that would make it clear who they had been, and who they had served, she left for every eye to see. She sent her puppet soldiers to return to their camps to make merry and let their presence be known to the world. When word of their demise spread, the priests of The Wilting Rose turned their eyes to the Heavens. They implored their Goddess to strike down the Abhorrent Queen before she could raise strength enough to retake their world.

The Goddess didn't hear their prayers. She could perceive nothing but Her newly formed foe. She wandered to the gates of Heaven as the Last Demon sauntered to the mouth of her own kingdom. She failed to notice the mortal eyes that fell upon Her. She peered past every other world to gaze upon the demon. Priests and witches beckoned for Her attention, knights gathered swords and awaited Her orders, the people of The Mortal Realm prayed for Her protection, for Her presence. Neither queen moved against the other. Neither queen dared walk past the edges of their empty realms. They simply looked at each other for a fleeting moment, and returned to their respective isolations.

Doll

The Wilting Rose pondered the best way to escape from the Heavens. She imagined shedding godhood and removing all the parts of Herself made divine by the throne of The High Heavens. She imagined slipping past the Garden of Nymphs where She was created, and leaving that piece of Her behind to feed the soil. Then She could escape to The Mortal Realm, to The Land of the Dead, to whatever fascinating space sits between realities. If She were to leave Her vessel behind, She'd need a new body. She needed something empty to store Her essence: something that wouldn't age or decay with Her inside. In the end, She found a perfect candidate. A porcelain doll—one the size of a mortal, with a rough resemblance to one as a bonus. It wore an expression of stoic sadness beneath perfectly painted makeup.

The Doll's limbs were slender and elegant, perfect for one used to the form of a Nymph. Its white hair fell delicately over its cheeks, just barely turning into curls at the tips. The dress it wore was a soft blue, with hints of pink to match its parasol—it had more ruffles and lace than

She knew what to do with, but She would learn. Its puffed sleeves and floor length skirt made Her feel like She could hide, that She could let Herself sink comfortably into it and travel as a stranger. She draped it with jewelry and flower petals, She fit it into Her favorite heels, and She prepared to let it become Her. She draped Herself over Her throne, with the Doll sitting in a ritual circle before Her. The candles lit with a soft pink flame, the symbols painted beneath it pulled themselves off the ground and began to float in rhythm with The Goddess's words.

First, She placed Her hope within it. Then She gave it Her love of games, Her love of dance, Her weakness for things that were shiny and beautiful at first glance. She gave it Her laughter and the way Her eyes lit up when something reminded Her of home. She gave it Her earliest memories—memories of discovering honey and tea—memories of Her first lover in the garden. She placed every part of Herself that was silly, trivial, and familiar into the Doll—the only things She wanted to take with Her. Finally, She prepared to let Her soul escape. Her chest grew light as the deepest and truest part of Herself rose within Her. It was freeing, for a moment, to feel the weight of divinity resting solely on Her back. To feel it as something She could leave drooping on the throne while She frolicked and forgot Her despair.

Her soul traveled to Her mouth and sat in the open air for only a moment. Before She let it loose, Her mind wandered to the future—a future where someone else made their way to the palace of The High Heavens—where man or monster finds a way to seize the essence She abandoned and rebuilt the world in their image. She imagined the essence itself decaying, or turning into an empty, undead thing. Too many images flooded Her mind to remind Her why She'd seized the essence of every god for Herself. Without hesitation, She swallowed Her soul back to the depths of Her wilting body. The hovering symbols crashed to the ground as smudged paint, the candles dulled until they were wisps of smoke and puddles of wax, the Doll sat lifeless on the palace floor. The Wilting Rose fled to Her chambers and wept. She wept for Her failure, for the reasons She could never leave, and for things She couldn't remember. She felt some loss of joy as She felt Herself deprived of sensations and tastes. Lovers and games appeared for one final glimpse before vanishing from Her sight. She grasped for these pieces of Herself, but they were gone, and She couldn't remember why.

The Goddess didn't hear the giggle that echoed through the throne room. A being sat daintily atop the throne of The High Heavens. A being with a stolen laugh and a desire to play games that she remembered, but had never truly played. A being who held so many wants and needs, but lacked an identity to give them context. The Doll longed for fun, love, and a sense of purpose—for anything that would help her feel like the person she'd been born to hold. And so she sat upon the throne that felt like hers. She kicked her fragile legs out, and waited for something to grab her attention. She waited for any sign of a life to make her own.

Daughter of The Rose

There was a time when creation didn't weigh so heavily on The Wilting Rose. When She first attained divinity, She let Herself become lost indulging in Her vision for the future of living beings. She wanted to try Her hand at making something with breath, something that She could sculpt with Her own two hands. She started by gathering the skeletons of primordials. The first dragon, whom the gods had split in two to steal fire from her belly, and the mountain traveler—a towering ram whose glimmering ore hooves had sculpted the mountains. The gods had poached the ram to steal its hooves, from which they gave their favorite human kings gold and silver. She had tried resurrecting them during the war, but too few pieces had been recovered. She had discovered the left half of the dragon along with its back-right leg, and of the mountain traveler she had only found fractions of its skull and a single hoofless leg.

She may have failed to bring them to life, but She could use them as the foundation for something new. She stitched them together with vines drawn from Her own veins. She let them curl from Her wrists to bridge the gaps in the mismatched skeleton. They expanded until they overtook the bones and offered a layer of soft green skin. The Goddess took a cluster of Roses from the Garden of the Nymphs and planted them within its eyes in the hopes that they could be its brain, that the same soil that She had emerged from could foster life again. She adorned Her creation in the jewels of The High Heavens. Enchanted bracelets pilfered from conquered temples were clasped around the dragon's horn. One massive sparkling necklace was wrapped around the ram's. Finally, She gave it life. She poured Her breath into her jaws, She beckoned her to wake and meet her mother.

When Her first creation rose to her feet she could barely stand. Her stump of a goat's leg struggled to cooperate with the massive talons of the dragon. Her leaf-green flesh expanded as she flexed her chlorophyll filled muscles. She struggled to move through the streets of The High Heavens as she stumbled towards her creator. The Goddess Roses' first work was ridiculous. Her body threatened to collapse under the weight of her bones. Her skin nearly burst as she brushed against jagged temple edges. Anyone else would have called her a failed first attempt and split her apart to make something useful. She looked like a child's drawing with her clashing horns and mismatched leg. The Goddess of Roses beheld Her creation, and She saw that she was perfect. She marveled at what She had done as Her arms wrapped around her lopsided head. She blessed the creature as Her first daughter. She told her everything about Herself, about Her home, and about the life that they would live.

For a time, Her creation kept Her from withering. They wandered through The High Heavens planting flowers. They visited the garden that had cultivated the soil that had birthed them both. She even took her down to The Realm of Mortals once, to see the mountains and the flames that had come from her skeleton. Few others seemed to see her beauty. Nymphs stifled laughs, and humans fled in terror. The Goddess paid them no mind. It didn't matter who else loved Her creation. She knew that she was good—that she was the spawn of Her heart. Her affection only began to fade as reality around Her turned to rot. When She began to notice the monsters that had spilled from Her, She struggled not to think of Her daughter as one of them. As it became clearer and clearer that She had poisoned The Realm of Mortals, She started to loathe anything that had spawned from Her imagination. She began to resent the creature that followed Her every footstep—the mess of vines with Her flowers blooming in her eyes that sat at the foot of Her throne and lingered just beyond Her bedchamber. She began to notice the way that it moved, the way that shreds of its body hung off of buildings it had crashed into. She had failed. Even Her first creation was a disaster.

In a moment of utter despair, She contemplated killing it. She imagined drawing the primordial bones from its cadaver and trying one final time to bring back the great beasts. The thought, however fleeting, horrified The Wilting Rose. She couldn't bring Herself to snuff Her daughter's life, but She couldn't have it near. And so, She sent Her creation on a quest. She sent it into the stars, to plant a bed of roses that would be visible from both The High Heavens and The Mortal Realm. Her creation, eager for an opportunity to make its mother smile again, sprinted clumsily along the lines between realms. It found itself between the stars, and let its breath spread across the void. The Wilting Rose urged it on. She begged it to plant flowers that could rival the size of worlds. The creature exhaled rosebuds until its breath grew thin, until it was surrounded by roses the size of the moon.

The creature was given no rest. The Wilting Rose bid it to continue. It continued planting beyond the sun, beyond the celestial bodies visible from The Mortal Realm. It pushed itself on until it had planted a flower in the center of every star. Only then, did Her first creation realize how far it had wandered from home.

The creature could no longer see the gates of The High Heavens. It could no longer hear its creator's voice imploring it to venture forward. It could no longer see anything but distant stars and drifting flowers floating around it in the empty void. The Goddess's daughter began to rush home, before realizing that it didn't know the way. It tried to follow the trail of its rosebuds, but they had scattered so far that it was impossible to determine where they'd come from. It wandered on, scouring the void for any sign of Her, until its body grew too weak to stand. It collapsed upon itself, too feeble to hold its skeleton. It couldn't move, it couldn't breathe, but it couldn't die either. As its body drifted among the stars, it held out hope that it would find itself back at the foot of The Goddess's throne. It knew that She would welcome it home, that She would wrap Her arms around her head as She once had. If she drifted long enough, surely she would close the distance. Surely She was looking for Her lost daughter, and when she drifted within Her line of sight, She would bring her home.

One More Chance

The Goddess of Roses raged through The Desert of Time. She destroyed any servant of the primordial keeper that crossed Her path. Her warrior spirit had been reignited as She'd realized what final chance She had to save Her reality, and She found no mercy for anyone who sought to slow Her down. The Goddess carved a bloody path to the winding steps of the primordial's tower. She sprinted up the stairway for what felt like millennia—unwilling to pause when Her body legs began to burn with exhaustion—unwilling to stop even to breathe. Eventually, the nigh eternal climb ended. The Goddess found Herself before The Keeper of Forward Movement. Their bottom half was that of a massive serpent covered in eyes. Following the serpent up to the Keeper's torso revealed a beast with the features of a burrowing rodent. The snake's mouth bit into its abdomen, its teeth formed the exposed ribs of the rodent that looked upon Her with eyes too wise and aware for any animals—the eyes of a being more powerful than divinity itself.

The Wilting Rose approached the being and demanded its favor. She implored the Keeper to send Her back to the beginning, to the final struggle in Her war against the gods. She told it of the decay of the realms—of the calamity She had allowed to pass. She knew if She'd had more time, She would have set reality right. She would have taken The High Heavens swiftly and comfortably, She wouldn't have fallen into despair, She'd have left the world free of evil and pain and subjugation. All She needed was one last attempt. An extra day, even an extra hour could be the difference between the reality She knew She was meant to make, and the despair of the one She had.

The Keeper was unmoved. They denied The Goddess's request, and bid Her to return to Her palace among the stars. This made Her furious. She demanded to know what reason they had for letting the reality they were meant to keep on its steady course get so far away from itself. She demanded to know why the Keeper refused to help Her, why they seemed not to care for the thousands who suffered and died by Her hand. The Keeper told Her that they had cared very much once. They had entertained Her story of a fluke in the flow of time, a grain out of place in the sands of time. But when they had granted

Her request, when they had sent Her back to fix Her mistakes, She hadn't changed a thing.

The Wilting Rose refused to be taken aback by this information. She insisted that it had been the same stroke of bad luck—that it was the Keeper's responsibility to identify what had gone wrong. Together, they could fix it, and then She could be returned to Her proper place. Again, the Keeper was unmoved. They did not respond to Her pleas for help, nor Her accusations of neglect on their part. They were prepared to ignore Her entirely until She gave up and went away. They were prepared to ignore Her, at least, until The Goddess moved Her blade against the Keeper's throat. The Keeper offered The Wilting Rose a challenge: they would comply with Her request only if She could answer a question. If She could approach their query with courage and truth, then they would move reality back as far along its journey through the desert as She wanted. The Goddess agreed, and so the Keeper asked Her: what would She do differently? What single thing would She change to make Her life as right and noble as it was destined to be?

Now The Wilting Rose was taken aback. Her sword fell as limp as Her tongue as She stared

into the wise and tired eyes of the Keeper. She
pictured a world without the monsters She'd
made. She pictured a world where She danced
and drank with Her sisters, where She sat among
mortals and remembered their shared victories
of gods, demons, and what aberrations appeared
under Her reign. She could see it so clearly in
Her head, as clearly as the days when She'd
almost had it. She knew that it was real, that it
was the destiny of Her reality, but She could not
answer the Keeper's question. And as She
looked into the eyes of the primordial, even as
they faced death and the crumbling of their
domain, She knew they could not answer either.

Night Light

There is something at the edge of my sight, something larger than any beast or demon in my records—perhaps sight is the wrong word—perhaps there is a feeling larger than anything I have ever felt. Something that lurks beyond my sight, beyond the sky, beyond The High Heavens itself. Something colder than frostbite, cold like the sun is hot: in overbearing waves, in a suffocating blanket of frigid night… One cannot describe its body, for it is far too large to be perceived. One can simply feel the sharpness of its teeth, the rumbling that shakes galaxies when its limbs reach across the cosmos. One can feel its eyes fall upon them, and know that it is oblivion. It is too precise, too focused, to be a celestial body. Though it rivals galaxies in size, it has intentions, it has hunger. It longs for anything warm, for anything loud and bright and interesting. Planets crumble as its shadow looms over them. The shards of worlds disappear as it searches them for life. Stars dull themselves to a tepid flame to avoid the fangs that would pop them like berries.

So distant a foe should be no cause for concern. It is a universe apart from us. It is a beast that few can perceive. And yet, the terror it has planted in me is unending. It holds my attention and my despair like no other. To feel its vision on me would be enough to drive me to the brink of madness, but I feel something far worse. I feel it looking past me to the ground beneath my feet. It is attracted to our lights—to fire and lightning and the flash of cannons. Its ears perk up at the ringing of hammers and trumpets. We pique its curiosity, for we are louder and larger than anything it has seen crawling across dirt. We project beacons into the night sky and scream prayers to the Heavens, and it has noticed us. It has become fascinated by us—it has begun its crawl to inspect these distinctly human traits, to have them for its lunch.

I begged for anyone to listen to me—to look into the sky and feel its eyes upon us. I screamed of it in the town square. I described what I could to priests and paladins in the hope that they would rally the people, that they would heed my warning to douse lights and silence steel. I have been cursed as a madwoman by some, looked upon with pity by others, but the result is the same: I am alone in my struggle. In a moment of desperation, I turned to The Wilting Rose, to

The Goddess who presides over this wretched world. I fell to my knees and begged Her to help me, or to show me an escape. She'd given me the sight to behold Her, to behold this ravenous thing at the edge of our universe. Surely She could face it, surely She could see it too.

I let my sight wander to the heavens, to the chambers of my withering queen. I saw Her gazing up into the sky. I saw Her gazing up into the monster. Her expression wasn't one of terror or rage, She wasn't twisted into knots over this unraveling entity. Instead, I watched Her mouth curl into a soft smile. Her eyes were glowing with comfortable sorrow as they searched for that same being that I dreaded to face. She let Her eyes fix on its presence, on the blanket of frigid oblivion, and She settled down to rest. She let its visage lull Her into sleep with the comfortable reminder that all of this will end. That this world She's failed to save will be welcomed into the same dreamless sleep She fell into at that moment.

Creature in the Temple Pit

The sight that She had given me weighed too heavily. I had seen too much—beheld too many monsters, and been first witness to the deepest flaws of divinity. I found myself alone. Few would listen to my ramblings, and those who believed me could hardly conjure care for the world that had destroyed them. I was left raving in a corner—waiting to be ushered away by whatever priest or city guard found me first. And so, I ran away. I fled from cities besieged by abominations. Corrupted nobles and charlatans of the faith became a distant memory. Specters trailed behind me, for a time: the ghosts of those I'd watched be torn apart who I'd captured as scribbled entries in my catalog as they were disemboweled. But eventually, even they failed to follow me. I ran beyond where they could wander. I found myself at the last true temple—at Her first temple: The Covenstead of Her Faithful Witches.

The Rosebud Coven had seen better days. They'd become thin in numbers and thinner still in allies. Their rations dwindled as they fought to encourage their garden to spring again. They nursed wounds dealt by soldiers who had once followed them into the jaws of death. They were

beaten, alone, and destined to be driven mad—or
die resisting insanity's call. Perhaps their despair
was why I found them perfect company; perhaps
it was why I fell to my knees and begged them
to take me in. They brought me into what
remained of their house and I told them my
story. I told them of the parasite that infected my
mind, of the monsters that I'd observed, of the
sins of The Wilting Rose. I waited for scorn, for
doubt, for a dagger in my belly for insulting Her
oldest and most loving followers. Instead, they
asked me what I needed. They offered tonics to
ease my pain, to slow the arrival of ghosts in my
eyes. I asked if they could remove the parasite,
but they could not. So I asked them if they could
kill me. I asked for poison stronger than the
monster clinging to my mind—poison that
would take me quietly into a final slumber.

At first, the head of their order offered me no
words. I was given a sad smile and a cup of tea.
Then, she asked for a peculiar favor: she asked
me to follow her beneath the Covenstead, down
into the depths of a cellar that predated the
witch's order. She pointed downward to our
supposed destination, but my eyes were drawn
to the ceiling above—to the shaft of light that
poured from a creature sized hole. A hole that
reeked of Her essence, of the bile that had

birthed my madness. I laughed as I let my eyes wander between the witch and the broken ceiling—of course, this was to be my demise: one final monster—one final flaw for my wretched book. The coven leader's eyes were unchanged. She waited patiently for my answer, never letting her hand so much as tremble as she pointed to the stairs, stained with the ooze of Heaven's final monster.

I complied in the end. I followed her down the slippery steps. I followed her into a moss covered chamber, dimly lit by fading lanterns. I was practically gleeful as I awaited the punchline. As I waited to see what beast would be my undoing, what monster would prove itself too much for even a woman who had seen every awful thing that had festered in reality's palm. I could never have prepared myself for the sight that awaited me. The creature was dangled upside down in the mouth of a long emptied well. It looked like a being of The High Heavens, like a long forgotten servant of divinity had been left to starve in a pitch black basement. It appeared to have massive petals arranged on its back, like the wings of the great messengers of the former gods. But these petals were flightless. They were brown around the edges and drooped onto the creature's emaciated shoulders. Its skin was sickly pale, as if it had spent its life some other vibrant color, only to settle on a faded, translucent form for its final moments. Its body was brightened only by the web of veins that ran across it in deep crimson. The sluggish flow of blood was visible even from a distance.

More disturbing than its veins was the substance they seemed to leak: crimson tendrils reached from the creature's twig-thin wrists like gelatinous blood torn from its wretched body. They reached beyond the crumbling edges of the well and into the hands of straining witches who kept the creature suspended in place. Similar tendrils poured from its eyes, clear and crimson spiraled together into arms stretched thin by the coven's embrace. Its body was leaking slime-covered limbs: saliva from screams unheard, phlegm from snot-ridden sobs, blood from every orifice. The wretched sight left the Rosebud Coven unphased. Their leader hardly had to urge them on. Each woman grasped on even as the creature struggled—even as it tried to throw itself deeper into the lightless abyss.

Sickness boiled in my belly as I beheld the kindness they shared with the wretched thing. Poison brewed in my heart as I watched them

bleed, as their arms threatened to splinter, to pull
free from their sockets and tumble into the well.
I could hardly stomach asking them why, but
they read the question on my contorted face.
They explained to me that this thing—this piece
of Her radiant essence graced them from The
High Heavens. They tried to bring it comfort, to
give it a welcome suiting divinity, but that only
worsened its mood. It had dragged itself below
the building. It had attempted to drive itself into
the Earth. All they could do to keep it alive was
hold on. All they could do was stop the worst
from happening—stop it from destroying itself.

The bile it carried within its body was more
potent than anything I'd encountered. This
creature held more than just a tear, a thought, a
wish whispered in the dark. This creature carried
Her heart. She'd cast Herself away—She'd sent
Her core to die. This was it: the only chance for
my suffering to end. If salvation was possible for
The Mortal Realm, this was it. I begged them to
let it go, to let Her have Her wish… They
refused. Denial made my skin grow hot, made
the sickness rage up to my throat. It was what
She wanted, what She needed—what We
needed. Still, the Rosebud Coven refused Our
request. We could not accept this. We could not
find relief without death. We told them as much,

but they continued to hold on—even as I shook
them, even as I pushed the creature's feet further
into the well. They stood firm. They whispered
prayers to The Wilting Rose. Not prayers for
mercy, for gifts, for anything meant for mortal
hands. They offered prayers of healing. They
urged The Goddess to give Herself mercy. They
urged Us to wait out the storm.

We could not understand their wishes. We could
hardly understand their words. Despair was all
consuming. Lines of bile ran from Our
mouth—from Our mouths? Still, the Rosebud
Coven held us tight. Their leader embraced Our
standing body, while the witches stopped Our
falling one. We could not accept this. We could
not accept their prayers, and yet, We had no
choice. They would not let Us go. They would
not let Us choose Our path. We would be forced
to dangle, as long as they wanted Us. Why did
they want Us? Why did they want Her? Why did
She keep Me? We may never know the reason,
but they loved Us, they wanted Us to stay. And
so We would. We would stay to finish our book,
and We would remain in the palace among the
stars. Until they let Us go, or the answers
become clear, and We begin to draw Ourselves
from the depths of Our first and favorite house.